Israel Washburn

Dedication of the Soldiers' Monument at Cherryfield, Maine,

July 4, 1874

Israel Washburn

Dedication of the Soldiers' Monument at Cherryfield, Maine, July 4, 1874

ISBN/EAN: 9783337136116

Printed in Europe, USA, Canada, Australia, Japan

Cover: Foto ©ninafisch / pixelio.de

More available books at **www.hansebooks.com**

SOLDIERS' MONUMENT

AT

CHERRYFIELD, MAINE,

JULY 4, 1874.

———

How sleep the brave, who sink to rest,
By all their country's wishes blessed!
When Spring, with dewy fingers cold,
Returns to deck their hallowed mould,
She there shall dress a sweeter sod
Than Fancy's feet have ever trod.

By fairy hands their knell is rung;
By forms unseen their dirge is sung;
There Honor comes a pilgrim gray,
To bless the turf that wraps their clay;
And Freedom shall a while repair,
To dwell a weeping hermit there!

———

PORTLAND:

BAILEY & NOYES.

1874.

SOLDIERS' MONUMENT.

THE citizens of Cherryfield, desirous of performing a duty incumbent upon them, at their annual meeting, March 30th, 1874, voted, "That the town raise $1,200 to purchase a soldiers' monument, and a lot upon which to erect the same."

They also voted to raise a committee to purchase and erect the same. Caleb Tracy, Esq., Hon. Alex. Campbell, and Hon. James A. Milliken constituted the committee.

This committee, after careful examination of designs, had a monument made similar to the one erected in Mount Hope Cemetery, Bangor. The work was done by S. P. Bradbury, Esq., of Bangor.

The material is Italian marble. Its height is seventeen feet, and the base is five feet square. On one face of the die is sculptured a broad shield surmounted by the arms of the different branches of the United States Service, and

draped with gracefully arranged flags, all in bold relief.   On
the shield is the following inscription in raised letters:

IN MEMORY OF THE

CITIZEN SOLDIERS OF THE TOWN OF CHERRYFIELD

WHO LOST THEIR LIVES IN THE

WAR FOR SUBDUING THE REBELLION OF

1861–5.

On the other three faces of the die are cut the names of
Brig. Gen. Hiram Burnham and fifty-three other soldiers.

The site selected for the monument is in Pine Grove
Cemetery, on a hill overlooking the valley of the Narra-
guagus.

The dedication took place on the 4th of July, A. D. 1874,
in the presence of a very large concourse of people from
Cherryfield and the neighboring towns.

The dedicatory exercises were as follows :

MUSIC BY THE CHERRYFIELD BAND.

SINGING OF A DEDICATORY HYMN BY A SELECT CHOIR.

UNVEILING OF THE MONUMENT.

HARRISON HUME, Esq., President of the Day, made the
following remarks and announced the order of exercises:

Fellow Citizens : We have assembled to-day not only to

celebrate the anniversary of our country's independence, but to perform a more sacred duty,—that of dedicating a monument to our dead soldiers.

The patriot fathers established for us a government of Liberty and Law. These men gave their lives to maintain it. To-day we endeavor to show our appreciation of the sacrifice they made by placing their names upon enduring marble.

THE REPORT OF THE MONUMENTAL COMMITTEE, BY HON. JAMES A. MILLIKEN.

Judge Milliken then made the following report of the proceedings of the committee, and presented the monument to the selectmen and inhabitants of Cherryfield:

Mr. Chairman and Gentlemen Selectmen: At the annual meeting in March last, the town of Cherryfield voted to erect a monument in memory of the citizen soldiers of the town who lost their lives in the War for the Union of 1861–5; and they elected a committee to purchase the monument and a site upon which to erect it. That committee gave prompt attention to the duty assigned to them and have already reported to the town, in special meeting, so far as relates to the selection and purchase of a lot and the cost of the monument. And now, Mr. Chairman and Gentlemen, I am authorized by the committee to present to you, and through you, to the inhabitants of Cherryfield, as our final report, the beautiful structure now first unveiled to their view. In size it may not meet the expectations of some; but we have no doubt that when its chaste design, fine proportions and artistic finish are considered, in connection with the intrinsic value of the imported material, and also the great amount of lettering upon it, there will be felt and expressed a general satisfaction with the manner in which the gentleman contracting to furnish the monument has discharged his obligation. It needs not that the committee should say that the work is well or ill done. There it stands and speaks for itself. Though modest in height and proportions, we think it not an unworthy testimonial of the people of the town to the valor and patriotism of those whose names are cut into its enduring substance. In selecting a site for its erection, the committee were governed by considerations of the design of the structure and the fitness of the surroundings. Erected by the living to the memory of the dead, it is intended to testify to generations yet to come, that the men who loved country and liberty and good government so well as to give their lives for these inestimable blessings, were held in grateful remembrance and appreciation by their surviving contemporaries. True, the mortal remains of the brave dead moulder not beneath it,—but few of them lie near it. The turf above their heads is made green by the dews that weep under the soft skies of Virginia and the Carolinas, and by the still waters of Georgia and Louisiana. The comrades who laid them away in the earth had no time

nor opportunity to set up even the frailest token to indicate
name or age, or place of rest.

> "Slowly and sadly they laid them down
> From the field of their fame fresh and gory;
> They carved not a line, they raised not a stone,
> But left them alone in their glory."

What more fitting, then, than that the stone erected to
their memory, at home, should stand in this "field of the
dead," this spot set apart and made sacred for the repose of
the loved and lost?

When budding infancy and prattling childhood come here,
led by the parental hand, to strew flowers upon the grave of
father, brother, or sister,—when youth and maiden, in the
flush of health and hope, walk these paths and read the names
upon the many white headstones, that have been and shall be
erected here,—when those in the full strength of life's prime
come here to

> "Muse a while on transient life's deceitful smile
> And death's long, dreamless sleep,—"

when the worn pilgrim of many years and many sorrows,
just ready to put off his sandals and lay aside his staff, and
lie down to rest, comes here to read once more the names
and recall the memory of those long gone before,—to each
and all of these shall these simple blocks and shaft be an
admonition and a reminder,—an admonition to be unselfish
and true and devoted as were they for whom these stones

were carved and set up and a reminder that they only are
held in grateful remembrance who have worked and sacri-
ficed and suffered for their kind or their country.

ACCEPTANCE OF THE MONUMENT BY THE TOWN AUTHORITIES.

In their name and behalf Samuel F. Adams, Esq., said:

Gentlemen of the Committee: The work to which you
were appointed, in procuring and erecting this beautiful
monument to the brave men of Cherryfield, who went forth
at their country's call, and gave up their lives, has been accomplished.   In accepting this noble work of art from your
hands, which now stands, for the first time, unveiled to public view, I can but express the proud satisfaction of our citizens. Its beautiful design, elaborate and fine finish, must ex-
ceed the expectation of all to whom it is of interest.

The care and protection of this memorial column will be a
part of the duty of the municipal officers of the town, aided
by the proprietors of this cemetery, which will give double
assurance of the performance of those duties which are
often sadly neglected by town authorities.

When the stricken friends of the soldier seek communion
with the spirits of the departed loved ones, what more fitting place can be found than this beautiful cemetery? Stand-
ing in this sacred place, amid these silent graves, contem-
plating the sorrows of the mourning heart, my thoughts are
turned to those of another who says: " The love that sur-

vives the tomb is one of the noblest attributes of the soul. It has its woes, it likewise has its delights; and when the overwhelming burst of grief is calmed into the gentle tear of recollection, when the sudden anguish and convulsive agony over the present ruins of all that we most loved, is softened away into pensive meditation on all that it was in the days of its loveliness, who would root out such a sorrow from the heart? Though it sometimes throws a passing cloud over the bright hour of gayety or spreads a deeper sadness over the hour of gloom, yet who would exchange it even for the songs of pleasure or the bursts of revelry? No, there is a voice from the dead sweeter than song, there is a remembrance of the dead to which we turn even from the charms of the living.

Oh! the grave! the grave! it buries every error, covers every defect, extinguishes every resentment; from its peaceful bosom spring none but fond regrets and tender recollections."

With feelings like these, then, I say, in this retired spot, amid these decorated mounds, by the side of this heavenward-pointing column, consecrated to our soldier-dead, we may find a fitting place for the sorrowing heart to meditate, and seek sweet consolation with spirits of departed loved ones.

Weave now garlands of sweet-scented flowers and strew them about this noble monument to the heroic dead to console the tender spirits of those who mourn, as only a " mother mourns for an infant that perishes like a blossom from her arms."

` Our Father who art in heaven, hallowed be Thy name. We feel it fitting that, at all times in every place, we should acknowledge Thee the giver of every good and perfect gift. In our sorrows and our joys, all that comes to us comes from Thee. We thank Thee for this day, for the privilege of meeting together. We thank Thee for the freedom we have, for the institutions we love, bequeathed to us by the men whose work we remember to day. For all their worth and worthiness we thank Thee. Especially do we thank Thee for the men whose noble deeds have perpetuated to us our institutions; the men who were willing to go forth and die for their country. We come to dedicate to their memory this monument, a memorial of worthy deeds; we dedicate it to the courage of men who were not afraid to die; we dedicate it to their devotion to their country, their self-denial and their death. We ask Thee that it may be a continual reminder to those who come after them of the worth of the institutions they enjoy. Grant, we pray Thee, that when the old, the middle-aged, and the young come here, they may remember that there is something better to live for, something better to die for than these material things about us; that lofty ideas, that worthy principles are more powerful and more enduring. We ask Thee to bless the families and friends of those whom we remember to-day in this act of dedication ; the fathers and the mothers, the sisters and the brothers, the wives and the children of those whose last remains lie on the hillsides and in the valleys far away from us. Thou knowest their needs. Supply, we pray Thee, their temporal wants ; watch over and care for them ; help them to bear their burdens ; be with them in their times of trial. Bestow upon them we pray, especially, every needed spiritual gift, leading them to Thyself. Wilt Thou, now, our Father, bless us who are here. As we remember the men who did so much that these institutions, these privileges we enjoy, might be perpetuated to us, may we consecrate our lives anew to duty. Increase in us a desire to do good work. May we be faithful. May we see something in life higher to live for than material things. May we be more inclined to reach out and strive after that which is true, that is pure, that is noble, that is worthy everywhere, until we shall come into the perfect man which is in Christ Jesus our Lord, which we ask for His name's sake, Amen.

The President then read the following letters in response to invitations to be present and participate in the exercises of the occasion.

LETTER OF GOV. DINGLEY.

LEWISTON, ME., July 3, 1874.

To W. M. Nash and others:

I have just returned after a few days absence and find the invitation to be with you on the Fourth.

It is too late now for me to reach Cherryfield, even did other engagements permit.

Accept my thanks for your cordial invitation and my best wishes for the success of your dedication and celebration.

NELSON DINGLEY, JR.

LETTER OF EX-GOV. CHAMBERLAIN.

BRUNSWICK, July 1, 1874.

Wm. M. Nash, Esq.—DEAR SIR:

I beg through you, as first named on the committee on the dedication of the Soldiers' Monument, to return my sincere thanks for the kind remembrance with which you honored me by your invitation.

It comes at a time when I am buried in business and cares here, so that I cannot allow myself the pleasure of sharing with you in this high and ennobling service of affection and patriotism.

Yours, with high regard,

JOSHUA L. CHAMBERLAIN.

LETTER OF EX-GOV. PERHAM.

PARIS, June 30, 1874.

W. M. Nash and others, Committee, etc.:

In answer to your communication of June 29th, I am compelled to say that an engagement, made some days since, makes it impossible for me to accept your kind invitation to be present with you on the coming Fourth of July. I am therefore obliged to forego the pleasure this occasion would afford me. With thanks for your invitation and regrets that I am unable to accept it,

I am, yours, very truly,

S. PERHAM.

LETTER OF HON. L. A. EMERY.

ELLSWORTH, June 30, 1874.

Mr. W. M. Nash and others, Committee:

Your very kind invitation to assist in the dedication of your Soldiers'

Monument the coming Fourth of July is received. It would give me much pleasure to participate in the exercises of such character, and I should especially enjoy meeting the good people of Cherryfield, whose hospitality is renowned, and whose spirit and zeal in all good works is manifest.

I fear, however, that the cares of business, and the expecting Mr. Hale's return, will prevent my having that pleasure this time.

I give you as a sentiment: Washington and Hancock; the one, the chief of the patriot army; the other, the chief of the patriot congress. May their linked names on the map be signs of liberty and country to the people of Eastern Maine.

Yours truly,

L. A. EMERY.

LETTER OF HON. SETH L. MILLIKEN.

BELFAST, June 30, 1874.

W. M. Nash and others, Committee, etc.:

I beg to thank you for the kind invitation extended to me to be present at the dedication of the Monument which you have erected in memory of the soldier citizens of your town, who fell in the war for the suppression of the rebellion. Be assured that I most heartily sympathize with the patriotic action of your people.

It is due to the heroic dead that they should be thus commemorated, and it is due to the living, especially to the young, that the great and virtuous actions of our countrymen should not be confined to the pages of history, to lie upon the library shelves of the student; but on enduring stone they should be written, that whosoever walks the public ways should have that which should bring them to mind and preserve their impressions upon the heart. Rome placed statues of those who had deserved well of their country in the baths, the groves, the forum and all prominent public places, and built many and magnificent monuments to commemorate the great deeds of the venerated departed. Greece lavishly, and in lines of never equalled beauty had done the same before her and taught her the valuable lesson.   Let us do likewise, well recollecting and realizing when we do it, that the victims of the great southern rebellion, whose graves roughen so many battle-fields, were martyrs not only to country but also to freedom.

Had I not already engaged to deliver an oration at Camden on the same day that your ceremonies are to occur I should certainly be with you in body as I am truly in heart.

I have the honor to be,

Your ob't servant,

SETH L. MILLIKEN.

ADDRESS BY

Ex-Gov. ISRAEL WASHBURN, Jr., of Portland.

Mr. President and Fellow Citizens :

Nine years ago to day, in commencing an address before the citizens of Portland, I said :

" This anniversary has a new place in our hearts and we come to its celebration as to a new heaven and a new earth. We seem to breathe the airs of an unfading spring; the sky bends above us with a kindlier smile and a sweeter love than we have known before.

> " ' A livelier emerald twinkles in the grass,
> A purer sapphire melts into the sea.'

" We have risen from the dreary wastes of slavery, from the dismal swamps whose atmosphere is heavy with murders, treasons and all abominations, to the broad and luminous table lands which are fanned by the healthful breezes of Freedom and Humanity. Henceforward in our commemoration of this day, our worship may be pure and our words sincere. No longer shall it be celebrated by mumbling the expressions

of a dead creed, but only by an honest recognition and a
faithful application of vital and practical truths."

And now, in opening this address it has occurred to me to
.inquire, how far these jubilant strains, these joyous and ex-
ultant notes have been justified by the events of the inter-
vening years. And I rejoice to say that, on the whole, there
is reason to believe that these peans of hope and triumph
were also the notes of prophecy. We *do* live in a better country than we had known, and have a nobler future than men
had anticipated, before.

With many mistakes and blunders there has been steady
and wholesome progress, not unaffected, it is true, by hinder-
ing influences, towards better things from that day to this.
By constitutional amendment and the amelioration of public
opinion, slavery has been made legally and practically impossible in this country—the slave of other days has been
recognized as a citizen, and his inalienable and fundamental
right of suffrage secured beyond danger of abridgement or
loss. He has taken his seat in the halls of legislation, State
and National. Schools and seminaries of learning have been
opened to him; the church receives him, and his claim to all
that man may claim has been allowed; for I regard the pass-
age of the civil rights bill as beyond doubt. His neighbor of
another race, so long his master and tyrant, has been enfran-
chised, too, and from a bondage scarcely less unhappy than his
own,—the bondage of prejudice, contemptuousness and in-

justice. All the States that were in rebellion have been successfully reconstructed, and avenues to prosperity, unknown and unhoped for in the earlier times, have been opened and are being rapidly occupied. A neighborly feeling—is not returning for it had never existed but—is growing up between North and South ; men of either section understand and respect each other, as they could not do so long as they were members of conflicting societies and warring civilizations. A common interest, a common sentiment and a common affection are nursing the pinions that, when stronger grown, shall bear both sections into a purer atmosphere—one in which all the elements of health, strength and expansion shall have easier play and ampler verge—than they had enjoyed before. Northern men and Southern meet upon the common ground of fellow-citizens, neighbors, friends ; concealments are unnecessary and confidences are unrestrained. The Vice-President of the Southern Confederacy resumes his seat in the House of Representatives, and in Henry Clay's old parlors in the National Hotel, beguiles the long evening hours with facts and recitals, showing how his section was maddened into rebellion by those who never meant it, but who for their own selfish ambitions played the game of fire-eating too recklessly and too long ; or by calling up recollections of what was most pleasant and genial, rather than what was most disagreeable and bitter during his long service and large acquaintance in Congress ; Robert Toombs, instead of coming to Bunker Hill to call the roll of his slaves, as he

2

once said he would do, visits General Grant, at the White House, and discovers that the President is a gentleman and a statesman ; Lucius Quintius Curtius Lamar, of Mississippi —of all the champions of Southern claims, erewhile the most uncompromising—lays a garland upon Charles Sumner's grave, so fragrant with love and tenderness that the wide and charmed air, filled with its sweetness, reaches every home and touches every heart from the Gulf to the Lakes.

O, friends! did we not in truth look upon a new heaven and a new earth on the first return of our great anniversary after that April day at Appomatox? Does it not seem almost like the fabric of a dream, the marvellous things that have been wrought in the nine years which connect this day with the fourth of July, 1865? When, in all the ages, in what land beneath the sun, was there ever a civil strife so fierce and terrible as that by which our country was torn and ravaged? And what nation ever returned so readily as ours has done to the arts and employments of peace and industry, after the convulsions of a protracted and exhausting civil war? In what land, were ever the wounds and cruel badges of battle so speedily healed over or removed?

May we not then conclude that the war was a mighty struggle of nature for the expulsion of a deep-rooted and deadly disease ; and that the treatment of the patient, in the stages of convalescence, though not at all times, perhaps, the wisest and best that could have been adopted, was more wise and successful than on the whole could have been reasonably expected, from any previous experience in analogous cases in the history of nations?

Surely, the 4th of July is neither an anachronism nor a blunder. It never meant nor suggested so much as it does to-day. Its atmosphere was never so clear, its airs never "so redolent of joy and strength." Never was there a year in which its celebration by rejoicings, by thanks, by prayers, by song and speech, by bells and guns, by processions and illuminations, was more fit, or more honorable to the instincts and feelings of an intelligent and faithful people than this.

You have coupled with the usual ceremonies of the day the dedication of a monument which your impulses of patriotism, gratitude, and affection have prompted you to erect in commemoration of the valor and devotion of the good and true men of Cherryfield, who in the great civil war, gave their lives for their country. In view of this fact, I have thought it not inappropriate to ask your attention at this time to the questions, "What do we owe these men and their comrades?" and "How shall we pay the debt?"

We owe to their valor, constancy, and faith, the preservation of the Union, the integrity of the nation, and the enjoyment of the rights of life, liberty, and the pursuit of happiness, to an extent and under a protection such as was never vouchsafed to any other people.

The ideas of the world in regard to government have

found expression in modifications of four primary and distinct
theories,—the theocratic, the autocratic, the aristocratic, and
the democratic.

Governments founded essentially upon one or another of
these theories, each borrowing something, perhaps, from the
others and clothing itself, at times, with forms, and impress-
ing into practical service functions which are not limited to
any one, as when the theocratic and autocratic theories take
on in practice patriarchal forms, or the aristocratic and democratic employ methods more or less republican, have existed
from the earliest ages of which we have any knowledge.

The variations, modifications, and experiments have been
infinite. The pure despotism, the limited monarchy, the
haughty oligarchy, the fierce democracy, in whatsoever essays
they had made prior to the discovery of America, towards
the best government, and with whatsoever modifications, had
each and all conspicuously failed to discover that which
should be satisfactory and final; that in which there should
be liberty, security, tranquility, and at the same time vigor
and life. Christianity, working after the laws that govern in
the realms of moral truth, slowly, painfully, through experiment, discipline, trial, experience and growth, was scarcely
felt for centuries in the moulding of society or the shaping of
government. Nay, it lent a new sacredness to power, in the
dogma of Divine Right; and mankind seemed bound more fast
than ever in the chains of a relentless absolutism. But this
doctrine of Divine Right once lodged in the thoughts of

men did, in the process of time, a work which its authors had not foreseen. The Calvinist, stern, logical, inflexible, accepting this dogma as the corollary of the Divine Sovereignty, built thereon as upon a foundation of adamant. He saw that the predicate of divine right must in politics be *natural right*; and that no government could be divine that did not recognize the claims of *humanity*. And note the wonderful providence! As if preparing for the advent of the great protestant reformers, who building better than they knew, invoked and marshalled forces that were to revolutionize, if not the religious, certainly the political ideas and fortunes of Christendom, Columbus, a son of the Catholic church, was moved by an inextinguishable impulse to search for a new world,—an undiscovered land slumbering in the bosom of the West,—the fortunate islands of ancient fable. And when the earnest and deedful puritan of that England,

> "Where girt with friend or foes,
> A man may speak the thing he will:"

already instructed by the writings of Milton, and Marvell and Sidney,—the grand old republicans of the times of the commonwealth,—that government was not made for one but all; that it rested upon the consent of all, and that such government and no other was of divine right—was told that far away in the west, removed from the obstructions and hindrances of European monarchies, a land of promise and of beauty, of virgin soil and genial sky, was waiting to receive

and welcome him, he delayed not to seek, occupy, and im-
prove it.

Divided by the Royal charters under which they were organized, into distinct and separate political communities,
though frequently embarrassed and vexed by the interfer-
ence of the home government, the colonists were generally
permitted to govern themselves; and for a century and a
half the right of self-government was exercised more fully
than it had ever been in any other country.

This education and experience were of incalculable value,
and when under the third George the exercise of this right
was interrupted, it was in the case of a people who knew
what it was and were prepared to defend it. And so these
men, entrenched in the divine right of human nature, did
not hesitate to brave and defy the power of what was the
mightiest nation on the globe,—a nation, as Daniel Webster
once said, " whose morning drum-beat following the sun
and keeping company with the hours, circles the earth daily
with one continuous and unbroken strain of the martial airs
of England."

In the struggle which ensued and which was protracted for
more than seven years, the independence of the colonies was
accomplished, and they became sovereign States. But a more
important and difficult labor than that by which independence
was effected through these years of fire and blood remained,
—the founding of a nation from these individual States. An
attempt at a common government, expressed in the articles

of the old confederation, was made and failed. Another, resulting in the Constitution of the United States, was successful. The government thus ordained and established was not theocratic, autocratic, aristocratic, nor was it purely democratic, for the last is practicable only in small communities, not in an extended and populous nation. Yet it was democratic in essence, but modified in form to suit the exigency ; it was a *representative Republic*, based upon equality of right and universal suffrage,—a marvel of wisdom, a miracle of fortune,—of all the achievements of human genius since the world began, the wisest, the noblest, the most beneficent, the most God-like. The wisest republican, the most sagacious democrat, the most learned and profound political thinker of Europe, would have pronounced as possible only a confederation of States, or a consolidated nation, and either would have been worthless. It was neither ; it was both. For all matters of ordinary local concern it was the former ; for all of general or national interest it was the latter, uniting in both cases the representative form and the democratic principle, and giving the only mode of government in an extended country, under which the liberties, the safety and the peace of the people could be secured. Had the government been a confederacy, it would have shared the fate of every similar form. Had it been a consolidated Republic,—all the States wiped out—who does not see how utterly impossible it would be to manage in one State forty millions of people occupying a domain so vast as ours ?

Suppose this territory were embraced in one State, or half a dozen States, there would be such a practical consolidation of powers in the one or in every one, such a centralization of forces, and agencies, as has postulated everywhere, and would infallibly bring in here, an amount of self-seeking and corruption that would sap the morals of the people and destroy the purity and vigor of the State. But with forty separate commonwealths, each supreme in its own sphere, but all subordinate to the general government in matters of common and national concern, no State is too unwieldly to be strong, none too insignificant to be secure. An outbreak or disturbance in one extends not beyond its own boundaries, and is easily checked and controlled by the central authority. While discontent may exist in one commonwealth, tranquility and order are seen in every other. A government like ours is stronger with twenty States than with ten, and stronger still with forty.

Had the old thirteen States expanded so as to include all that are now in the Union, the Union would long ago have fallen to pieces. The beauty and glory of this government inhere in the fact that it necessarily grows steadier and stronger with the entry of every new State that comes with due preparation into the Union.

Under this matchless government. the country grew rich and powerful, commerce was extended, manufactures were introduced, agriculture fostered, education was looked after, and religion, left to the people, became the ally of freedom and civilization. The progress of the country for three-quarters of a century, under the constitution, was the wonder of all nations.

But all this time a cancer of malignant type had been eating, with slow but gradually accelerated movement towards the vitals of the constitution. Chattel slavery demanded the possession of the government. It was so inconsistent with every idea and principle of the constitution, that men saw that such demand must be resisted, if the charter of our liberties was to be preserved. And so, unable to capture the government by the ballot, it resolved to destroy it by the sword.

Then it was that the patriotic men of that part of the country whose soil had never been polluted by this scourge, without distinction of party or respect to antecedents, resolved in their hearts that this nation should be preserved, whatever might be the cost of treasure or of blood. And well and proudly did they keep that vow. Whatever others may have done,—and how faithfully many stood and served, men and women, we all know,—the special saviors of the country were those who when the alarm was sounded, hurried to the camp and the battle field, leaving behind them the sweetest and most precious things in life,—the dear old home, the family, the trade or occupation which was its only support, and from a sense of duty and in a spirit of God-like sacrifice, the thought of which stirs in our hearts the finest emotions that kindle there, and brings to our eyes from their deep beds the holiest tears of gratitude, tendered the price-less offering of health and life in defence of liberty and native land. Many, O how many of them, sleep where no eye of wife or child or parent or loving friend, shall discover the place of their long repose! Yet not a grave in all that South land, in which a soldier of freedom has been laid away, but is "hallowed ground," or which to the patriot's eye of faith is not garlanded with amaranthine flowers, and in his grateful heart is not moistened by the dews of Heaven's sweetest and holiest love.

It is difficult, I think impossible, to fully realize the grandeur of the cause which they served. Aggregate every struggle for a thousand years in which a nation has been saved, and is it extravagant to say that in importance to the fortunes of civilization, they fade before that in which your neighbors fell?

Consider. This American government, this government of governments which I have described, this consummation towards which mankind had worked since the race began—the outgrowth and result of trials, guesses, speculations, agonies, defeats, hopes—this experiment which could be commenced only on a new continent, with a fair field and ample room, and for which, if it had not been inaugurated here, no other theatre could have been found on the round earth,—this sisterhood of republics, this commonwealth of free States, strengthened and guaranteed by its system of differences, checks, and balances,—this prophecy, it may be, of the coming time of which England's Laureate sung,

" When the war-drum throbbed no longer. and the battle flags were
    furled
In the Parliament of man. the Federation of the world"—

the gains of all the past, the hopes of all the future,—were saved to America and to mankind by the valor and devotion of our soldiers in the civil war.

And well and nobly, citizens of Cherryfield, did your town perform her part in that supreme hour of trial. Words can add nothing to the eloquence of the simple statement, that from a population of less than 1,800 souls fifty-four good and strong men laid down their lives for their country. Of these men I well remember one, truest of the true, strongest of the strong. My official duties in regard to the organization of his regiment brought me into near relation with Lt. Colonel, afterwards General Hiram Burnham. There was such native force, earnestness, directness and capacity in the character of this man that I never failed to derive strength and courage myself from his companionship.. Would that I could more worthily discharge the personal obligation, which I am glad to have this opportunity to acknowledge.

I feel that I have succeeded but imperfectly in this attempt to estimate the extent and fulness of the country's debt to the soldiers and sailors, to whom it owes its preservation. But any words, inadequate as they may be, which shall have the effect of turning your attention to this subject, will not have been spoken in vain.

And now, with your leave, I proceed to inquire, *How shall this debt be paid?*

The obligations of a grateful country to the soldiers and sailors, who defended and preserved it in its hour of extremity, are numerous and weighty, and many forms of recognition and payment are demanded. To those who fell, that which you employ to-day is beautiful, appropriate and tender.

"To live in hearts we leave behind is not to die."

To preserve the memory of the gallant dead by inscribing a record of their names and deeds upon enduring marble or granite, that may be read and known of men, and especially of those who bear their blood, alike in the present and the future age, is a tribute which the heart of mankind has never denied. The hope that we may be remembered with kindness and affection, when we shall have passed away, is a thoroughly human one, and is of practical value in its influence upon life.

" Victory or Westminster Abbey !" exclaimed Wolfe when moving to attack Quebec—and both were his.

But a solider recompense is made when those who were dear to them in life, are faithfully and kindly looked after and cared for by the country for whose sake they died.

The first duty of a nation is overlooked when those who have been deprived of their natural protectors, or those who have been themselves disabled in the country's defence, are treated with cold indifference, and left to suffer the stings of penury and want, which no act of theirs invited or could have averted.

The best that can be done in such cases is but a slight return for a priceless service. Republics have been charged with ingratitude. Be it ours to break the line of evil precedents, if such exists, and to convince the nations that justice and generosity are associated with true liberty.

The best payment, however, for such service,—the wisest and most practical discharge of duty, alike to the dead and the living, is when a people are vigilantly intent to show by their character and their works, that the country that was preserved, was worth saving; shall make the best practical use of the good that has been achieved for them. If the country by its wickedness or weakness is to fall, the sacrifice was in vain.

The war with its disturbing influences, the changes in habits and occupations it occasioned, its vast expenditures, its unavoidable employment of unworthy and selfish men at times, its relaxations in manners and morals, left an inheritance of many dangers. Soldiers of fortune, adventurers, and rascals, discover in the opportunities and tendencies of such seasons, manifold avenues to peculation and fraud, and they are swift to occupy them. While the patriotic and true are engrossed with the settlement of great questions, with vital necessities, with the duties of repair and restoration, the selfish and false are busy with their schemes of greed and plunder. Familiarity with large sums encourages a liberal arithmetic,—where the carcass is the vultures gather. When vast national expenditures are unavoidable corruption festers, and theft and plunder hold carnival; men become giddy, impatient, excited. They cannot wait for slow gains, or descend to small things. Details are pitiful, and the homely virtues disgusting. Industry is a joke, economy a by-word, and honesty a fool. Looseness in manners, profligacy in life, faithlessness to obligations become so familiar that they cease to shock or disquiet the average man and woman.

There is cause for alarm. Danger is everywhere—in business, in society, in the noiseless walks of private life, as well as on the wider theatre of public affairs.

Of what avail the sufferings and the sacrifices of the dreadful years from which we are so lately come, if these things are to go on? But they must not go on. The people must call a halt, and they will. Did I not believe it I should despair of the country. Economy, retrenchment, reform, responsibility, and purity must be the popular watchwords. The battle is a hard one. The enemy is strongly entrenched and has great facilities for mobilization, while the people are unorganized, undisciplined and unwieldy.

Your duty, gentlemen, as it is that of every man who really loves his country, and believes that under its admirable government it can be not only saved, but raised to higher and brighter levels of prosperity and honor than it has yet reached, is to warn and arouse your fellow citizens—to point out the perils which threaten them—the way of escape and to walk therein. The first great need is to educate the people to higher ideals of a true manhood and a genuine success. And before this can be accomplished they must be relieved of the false ideas and estimates which the glamour of a seeming but delusive prosperity and greatness, based upon pretence, sham, and fraud is apt to encourage. Our work is first and mainly at home, with ourselves and our ideals. Without right thinking we cannot expect wise acting. If we are slaves to wealth, extravagance, and show—if we look with foolish eyes upon their possessors and exhibitors as the fortunate and happy ones of earth, careless of the means by which they rose,—if we think that fraud and falsehood may be winked at when successful, we make reformation and improvement impossible. The work then must begin with the people and *now*. We are not to wait for better opportunities hereafter, or trust to great achievements by others. "Opportunity" was painted by the ancients as wearing her hair in front and as bald behind. She could be taken only by the forelock; when she had once passed it was forever too late. Let the present time be unimproved and the hour is not distant when the people will have become so thoroughly demoralized as to be unworthy and unsafe depositories of power. If there is any thing in Christianity, any verity in human history, it is certain that truth and right and conscience only are eternal,—that falsehood, injustice, and fraud, no matter how they may flourish for a season, are self-destructive and sure to fail in the end. In our own day we have seen many confirmations of these truths.

The delusive apparition of success, rising like an exhalation from the mire of corruption, vice and dishonesty, may flaunt itself in the face of the world for a season, and dazzle the eyes of the weak. Some reckless adventurer, some coarse voluptuary, or some arch swindler, may ride, for a time, on the top wave, of what goes for prosperity, but only to be miserably stranded at the last. He may have venal courts of justice, subsidized presses and purchased legisla tures to facilitate his robberies; but a day comes when his corrupt and flagitious practices serve him no longer. His railroads, steamboats and opera houses fall into other hands, his chariot is broken, Anonyma flouts, and the fiend he has served but too faithfully, mocks him. He disappears from the theatre on which he played so loud a part, and though he may be remembered for awhile, it will be to point a moral, not to adorn a tale. Fiske falls a victim to his own arts and at the hand of an associate, and Tweed dons the wardrobe of a felon.

Twenty-five years ago a giant lie was enacted in France. Her President, relying on his name and putative race, caused himself to be elected Emperor, although in his oath as President he had sworn to defend and preserve the Republic. A throne erected on perjury could be maintained only by kindred crimes; but such was the audacity and facility of the usurper that the probability of his fall, through an absence of such support, seemed slight indeed. By degrees all power was absorbed in the Emperor. The press was muzzled, the army corrupted, the church subsidized, the *bourgeoisie* were quieted with a factitious prosperity, and the *sans-culottes* were fed from the public crib. Paris was made more beautiful and splendid than ever. Princes, of the proudest and most ancient monachies of Europe, paid court to the new Cæsar, France was the first of nations, and NAPOLEON WAS FRANCE. Europe gazed, trembled and admired. He had won success, the world said ; but it was only that which the juggling fiend, who presides over falsehood, gives. He had labored for himself and not for his country. The hour of collapse struck at last. The throne of lies fell, and the arrogant and insatiate autocrat, whose nod had decided the fate of dynasties, appeared the imposter that he was. Detested for his crimes and loathed for his vices, a fugitive from his country,—a debauched people, a degraded nation, a dismantled capital, were the trophies of his career.

It is but a few years ago, and is within the remembrance of all observing men, that certain names in our business and political circles were prominent and dazzling, while old-fashioned people, common folks were nobodies, " slow coaches," " behind the times," " played out." Meet one of these new great men or one of his subalterns, and you would soon be made to understand that you were at a discount, if not an utter mistake. And so it was seen that these magnificents

3

were carrying things with a high hand. And the world wondered and cried "success!" But the hour of trial came; murder will out, and so will corruption and robbery. The mills of God "may grind slowly but they grind exceeding fine." Exposures began to be made; one led to another; one stone fell, then a column, then the whole wall, until this miserable but most pretentious fabric of venality and scoundrelism, built upon the sand of corruption, and not upon the everlasting granite of integrity and principle, is trembling to its fall. The shrines of the gods whom these men had served, and foolish people had worshiped, are breaking and tumbling, while the gods themselves of *Credit Mobilier* and kindred idolatries have been unmasked and disgraced.

Notwithstanding the patent evils and dangerous tendencies to which I have adverted, I am yet able to look out upon the country's future on this anniversary with hope, rather than despair—in the confidence that the people have the intelligence to see and understand the evils that beset them, and the strength to make such resistance as may be required for the preservation of their free and wholesome institutions.

In an address which I wish to be practical, I seek, rather than avoid the consideration of topics that are near at hand and the expression of thoughts that are trite so that they be timely and true. For our business is in the present and our duties are directly before us. The debt is due to-day and its payment cannot be postponed. We cannot deal with the needs and dangers of the next generation but we can with those of this. If we do what is required in 1874, 1875 will be relieved of tasks and burdens that might be too great for it to perform or bear.

Looking then to the questions that demand immediate attention, we see directly before us that of *reform in the civil service*. It is one of the most difficult problems before the country. How to secure faithful and efficient service; and how to hold the power of official patronage within due limitations and restraints, and yet keep up a wholesome interest in public affairs, are questions that have taxed the earnest and thoughtful consideration of the best minds in the country for many years. It is also a subject as vast as it is difficult. The appointees of the federal government are not as in the time of Andrew Jackson, a handful, but scores of thousands. There can be no question that one of the chief perils of the nation arises from the relations of the civil service to the country,—from the manner of its constitution, and the political or rather party work which an appointment to office is understood to imply by those in whose interest or by whose procurement it was made. It is a question that must grow into the first importance and continue to be agitated and discussed by intelligent and patriotic citizens until some practical and efficient solution has been reached, and it should be our purpose to give hospitable reception and a fair trial to every plan for reform that presents a reasonable promise that

it may be successful,—for it is only by practical tests, care-
fully and patiently applied, that the final discovery will be
made, and the needful reform effected.

Among the dangers too obvious to be overlooked, and
which should awaken the serious apprehension of the country, is that resulting from the general and apparently irresis-
tible tendency of things in the direction of *centralization*.

Educated in the specious school of the Virginia abstrac-
tionists, many men of acute rather than strong minds, specu-
lators and theorists—especially after the subtle intellect of
Mr. Calhoun discovered that the cause of slavery would be
served by it—became believers in, and champions of the dogma of State Rights; and so far did they go in their denials of
the legislative power of Congress, and in their restriction of
the functions of the general government, that their affirmative
and vehement claim of the right of any State, at any time
when it saw fit, to secede from the Union, was not only a
logical deduction from these positions, but its exercise, con-
ceding their soundness, would have been matter of but little
practical importance to the nation, stripped as it would have
been, of nearly every essential attribute of sovereignty.

These opinions, which, from their association with the
slavery controversy, were rapidly propagated, and came to
be widely held in all parts of the country, found their logical
expression in the attempt at secession, and in rebellion.

It will not seem strange that after such efforts as the country had occasion to make to put down a rebellion organized and pushed in the immediate interest of slavery, and on the theory of State Sovereignty, there should be a strong reaction towards power and centralization in the general government. There is unquestionably real danger that this movement of forces and tendencies to the centre, may go unchecked until all substantial power and authority shall be absorbed in the nation, and the States shorn of their most necessary practical functions.

I confess that I look upon the disposition of Congress to extend its jurisdiction over questions and concerns heretofore acknowledged by all parties, to pertain, rightfully and exclusively, to the States, with unaffected alarm. Congress is almost daily legislating upon matters, where the right would have been promptly, not to say indignantly, repudiated by such broad constructionists as Mr. Clay, Mr. Webster, Mr. Mangum, Mr. Evans, and Mr. Clayton.

The nation is becoming everything, the States nothing.

For all ills and evils, for all inconveniences and accidents, relief is sought at Washington..

Whatever State legislation, or individual or corporate enterprise and capital are inadequate to accomplish, or unwilling to undertake, the federal government is confidently asked to promote.

Among the most wholesome and effective means of staying this rapid and appalling march of centralization, will be the inflexible and persistent requirement by the people of the practice of *economy* and *retrenchment*. Necessary in themselves, they are indispensable to a true adjustment of the proper relations of the national and State governments to each other. Centralization, with its hundreds of millions for yearly disbursement, must breed carelessness and prodigality, while vast and loose expenditures feed and strengthen centralization. A terrible peril—insidious, fascinating, but inexorably fatal, lies in this source and reservoir of corruption, the Treasury. Fifty years ago, aside from the public debt, the entire payments of the government scarcely exceeded ten millions in a year, where now they are two hundred millions.

A strict limitation of appropriations to constitutional objects,—to cases where the power is clear and the necessity unquestionable, an educating of the people to the constant inquiry whether the appropriations are in all cases within the scope of congressional power, and to a vigilant scrutiny of details, with a practice of holding members to a rigid accountability for their votes, are duties in the performance of which the people may do much towards discharging their obligations to those who preserved for them the government under which they live. I have sometimes thought that a provision for the publication in the newspapers of the several States of all the items of appropriation and expenditure by authority of Congress, so explained in detail as to be easily understood, would be wise and salutary. It is, I imagine, only necessary to bring the attention of the people to these things and lead them into the habit of classifying and examining all items of expenditure, to effect a reform in the manner of dealing with the people's money that will largely protect the Treasury from spoliation, and the people from the arts and influences of corruption.

When our whole annual expenditure was less than thirteen millions, an administration was overthrown on the cry of "Retrenchment and Reform." That the administration of to-day is open to censure on the score of extravagance is what I am not aware has been seriously, or can be justly charged. That a practice of latitude reaching to looseness, has crept into the halls of legislation is what was, perhaps, to be expected from the circumstances and situation succeeding so great an overturn as was occasioned by the civil war. However this may be, we are now specially concerned with the present and the future—with the existing and probable examples, facilities, and tendencies in the line and direction of extravagance and corruption. Excuses that have been, or may be pleaded for the past, are irrelevant in respect to the future. Congress will be as economical, vigilant, and honest as the people demand that it shall be, and no more. The country is ruled by public opinion. All reform must have its impulse from the people. They are slow, patient, and long-suffering, but in this country have always been found sure and reliable in the end.

The country has of late been deeply moved by questions

regarding its *currency,* and it is matter of special confidence
and encouragement that in their discussion and treatment the
people have generally been steadier and wiser than their representatives.   In this State, however, I am happy to say that
representatives and people have stood together. Let the people firmly maintain their position, and the evils of a debased
currency will be swept away.   The time has come not merely
for firmness, but for aggressiveness.   Too long have the government and people suffered from absence of positive and ju-
dicious legislation—too long have they waited for a more fa-
vorable season, or for "something to turn up." Year by
year has industry been stayed, and capital timidly employed,
or in absence of legitimate demands, cast into the maddening
whirl of speculation. There was never a more costly delu-
sion than that a people could thrive upon a depreciated or
shifting currency. If there is any verity that is immutable
in the nature of things, or by the experience of mankind, it
is this, that there can be no such thing as prosperity based
upon lying. A currency that assumes to perform the office of
money, but which, instead of being money, is only a promise
to pay in another promise, is of all false pretenses one of the
most mischievous and impudent. It places the nation which
uses it at a disadvantage compared with the nations that re-
ject it. It practically pays a commission unknown where
payments are in the universal currency, on its purchases of
foreign commodities, and it submits to a discount on all its
sales abroad. There is, in my judgment, no duty more ur-

gent than that of replacing the sham representative of money, by which the country is continually deluded and cheated, by gold and silver or their exact equivalent.

Such, fellow-citizens, are some of our national evils and dangers. To say that they are not real and imminent, would be to deceive ourselves where deception is fatal. But that they may not be successfully met or flanked, I have already said I do not believe. And I have such faith in the essential soundness and vigor of the American people—a faith strengthened by their recent efforts to correct abuses on the part of their agents, and errors of their own, that I am not permitted to doubt that they will be. The demand so emphatic and earnest as to have been promptly respected, for the repeal of bad laws, the prosecution and disgrace of conspirators against the public funds, and betrayers of the country's trusts; the resolute and intelligent questioning of monopolies, are among the recent signs and tokens of a healthy spirit in the people which should go far to reassure and encourage us.

Mr. Greg, the author of "Enigmas of Life," is publishing in the Contemporary Review, a series of articles under the title of "Rocks Ahead," in which he states the conviction that there are three especial dangers hanging over the future of England. They are:

I. The political supremacy of the lower classes.

II. The approaching industrial decline of England.

III. The divorce of the intelligence of the country from its religion.

These dangers, if they truly exist, are, as it will be seen, deeper and more vital than any of those that have been mentioned as menacing the future of America, and I am happy to believe that here they are not of sufficient magnitude to occasion any serious apprehension. Our perils, compared with these, are minor and secondary, and *these* are not likely to seriously disturb us. Of the first I would say, we fear the supremacy of no class so long as all classes are in the enjoyment of political power. It is disfranchisement that implies danger. In regard to the second point, it may be remarked, that the only cause of apprehension of an industrial decline in the United States is to be found in the too general disposition of men and women to live without work, and by their wits. But in this country this evil is always working its own cure. As to the third specification, it is sufficient to observe, that the intelligence of the country, so far from divorcing itself from its religion, appears to be lifting her out of the unhealthy atmosphere in which she has been kept by ignorance and superstition.

From this brief and imperfect survey of the field, I return to the position from which we started, and report that from all I have discovered, my faith is strong and unshaken that the debt which this nation owes for its preservation, *will be faithfully paid.*

And, fellow-citizens, it is only by contributing your share towards its payment, that the chaste and noble monument that stands before us, becomes honorable to yourselves, and such a testimonial as is due to a patriotism than which the world has seen none more grand in what it accomplished, or more pure in the spirit by which it was inspired.

Accepting, then, the truth that this offering is fitly and worthily made in the spirit of sincere consecration of heart and life to the dutiesa nd responsibilities of citizens, and in no other way, let it be now dedicated to the memory of the gallant dead whose names it bears.

> " And let the blue sky overhead,
>   The green earth on which ye tread,
>   All that must eternal be
>   Witness the solemnity."

SINGING " AMERICA," BY THE ASSEMBLAGE.

BENEDICTION BY REV. MR. HOLYOKE.

APPENDIX.

NAMES ENGRAVED UPON THE MONUMENT.

Hiram Burnham, Brigadier General.
George H. Jacobs, Sergeant, Co. G, 6th Regiment.
Rufus Madden, Private, Co. G, 6th Regiment.
Lawrence O'Laughlin, Private, Co. G, 6th Regiment.
Alonzo C. Willey, Private, Co. G., 6th Regiment.
Thomas J. Small, Private, Co. G., 6th Regiment.
Joseph Y. Harrington, Private, Co. G, 6th Regiment.
David Quigley, Private, Co. G, 6th Regiment.
Sidney M. Tucker, Private, Co. G, 6th Regiment.
George W. Burnham, Captain, Co. G, 6th Regiment.
Mitchell Hunter, Private, Co. G, 6th Regiment.
William F. Burnham, Teamster, Co. C, 11th Regiment.
Edwin C. Haycock, Private, Co. C, 11th Regiment.
Benjamin D. Willey, Private, Co. C, 11th Regiment.
Samuel H. Whittaker, Private, Co. C, 11th Regiment.
Stillman Anderson, Private, Co. G, 11th Regiment.
Rufus Foss, Private, Co. I, 13th Regiment.

George H. Foss, Private, Co. I, 13th Regiment.
Everett Leighton, Private, Co. I, 13th Regiment.
Oscar C. Small, Private, Co. I, 13th Regiment.
Wm. McFarland, Private, Co. D, 2d U. S. S. S.
George H. Coffin, Sergeant, Co. D, 2d U. S. S. S.
George E. Nash, Sergeant, Co. D, 2d U. S. S. S.
Arthur W. Tucker, Private, Co. D, 2d U. S. S. S. } Twins.
Washington Tucker, Private, Co. D, 2d. U. S. S. S.
George M. Nash, Sergeant, Co. C, 2d Cavalry.
William R. Newenham, Lieut., Co. H, 1st Heavy Artillery.
Augustus C. Bond, Private, Co. H, 1st Heavy Artillery.
Samuel H. Buzzell, Private, Co. H, 1st Heavy Artillery.
Henry W. Grant, Private, Co. H, 1st Heavy Artillery.
James W. Wallace, Private, Co. H, 1st Heavy Artillery.
Warren C. Wallace, Private, Co. H, 1st Heavy Artillery.
Samuel Hart, Private, Co. H, 1st Heavy Artillery.
Lorenzo M. Coffin, Private, Co. H, 1st Heavy Artillery.
Wheelock Tucker, Private, Co. H, 1st Heavy Artillery.
Jerome Mitchell, Private, Co. I, 1st Heavy Artillery.
Daniel W. Tucker, Private, Co. I, 1st Heavy Artillery.
Albert Tucker, Private, Co. I, 1st Heavy Artillery.
John T. Quigley, Private, Co. G, 1st Heavy Artillery.
Henry E. Archer, Private, Co. K, 1st Heavy Artillery.
Ichabod W. Davis, Private, Co. B, 31st Regiment.
Abraham A. Madden, Private, Co. B, 31st Regiment.
John E. Dorr, Private, Co. B, 31st Regiment.
William H. Willey, Private, Co. B, 31st Regiment.
John McClusky, Private, Co. H, 31st Regiment.

Robert McAuley, Private, Co. H, 31st Regiment.

Aaron Tracy, Private, Co. K, 31st Regiment.

Loring W. Willey, Private, Co. A, 19th Regiment

James P. Shoppe, Private, Co. C, 28th Regiment.

Ammi C. Wilson, Corporal, Co. C, 28th Regiment.

Howard C. Leighton, Private, Co. D, 22d Regiment.

William A. Colson, Private, Co. D, 22d Regiment.

Samuel Conners, Private, Co. E, 1st Cavalry.

James R. Nickels, Captain, Co. I, 14 Conn. Vols.

www.ingramcontent.com/pod-product-compliance
Lightning Source LLC
Chambersburg PA
CBHW032123080426
42733CB00008B/1041